ABC's
OF YOU

Dominique Woodhouse

Columbus, Ohio

The views and opinions expressed in this book are solely those of the author and do not reflect the views or opinions of Gatekeeper Press. Gatekeeper Press is not to be held responsible for and expressly disclaims responsibility of the content herein.

ABC's of You

Published by Gatekeeper Press
2167 Stringtown Rd., Suite 109
Columbus, OH 43123-2989
www.GatekeeperPress.com

Copyright © 2022 by Dominique Woodhouse

All rights reserved. Neither this book, nor any parts within it may be sold or reproduced in any form or by any electronic or mechanical means, including information storage and retrieval systems, without permission in writing from the author. The only exception is by a reviewer, who may quote short excerpts in a review.

Library of Congress Control Number: 2022943582
ISBN (paperback): 9781662928796
eISBN: 9781662928802

FOREWORD

I wrote this book to help encourage, enlighten, and educate men, women, boys, and girls on the value of their life. Whether it be a minor battle or major struggle, internally or externally, they should know how important they are as an entire being. This book was inspired by those who suffer with depression; those who think that the world would be better without them; or those who believe that no longer existing would make the all the pain, uncertainty, and doubt go away. Love yourself inside and out. I wrote this for you. Read this on your toughest days to pull through, and even on your easiest to remind you. Read this as many times as you need to *keep going.*

For additional help and resources contact the **National Suicide Prevention Lifeline** at **988**.

A FOR
ALIVE

You are here. You are breathing. Let's keep it that way.

B FOR

BEAUTIFUL

You are
beautiful
from the
inside out.

C FOR

COURAGEOUS

You have faced and conquered so much.

D FOR
DESERVING

You deserve to be happy.

E FOR

EVOLVING

There will always be change; don't fear becoming your new, best you.

F FOR
FLAWED

Embrace things you can't change, for flawlessness is fiction.

G FOR

GIFTED

Find your gift and share it with the world.

H FOR

HELPFUL

Things turn out well for those who are helpful.

I FOR

IRREPLACEABLE

There will always, and only be, one you.

J FOR

JUTTING

You are boundless. There is nothing you can't get past.

K FOR

KEY

You are essential. Your existence is vital.

L FOR

LOVED

Someone loves you—
and you should too.

M FOR

MEANINGFUL

You have a purpose.

N FOR

NEEDED

This world needs you, and most importantly, you need you.

O FOR

OKAY

It's okay to
not be okay.
You are
human.

P FOR

PRICELESS

Know your worth and don't put a number on it.

Q FOR
QUALITY

You are one person with so much to give.

R FOR

RADIANT

There is no darkness that can overcome your light.

S FOR

STRONG

You are
strong
enough to
keep going.

T FOR
TENACIOUS

Through all your pain you've managed to keep going; DON'T STOP.

U FOR

UNIQUE

There is only one you. You cannot be replaced.

V FOR

VALIANT

Even with obstacles like doubts and fears, your bravery got you here.

W FOR

WORTHY

You are deserving of greatness.

X FOR

X

"X" out every negative thought you have about yourself.

Y FOR
YOU

You deserve love, happiness, and second chances.

Z FOR
ZERO

You have
zero reasons
to give up
now.

I hope after reading this book that it makes you want to dance, smile, laugh, cry tears of joy—but most importantly—LIVE. I made this book pocket-sized so that you can read it as many times as you need; *whenever* and *wherever* you need. Use the following pages to write down songs, quotes, inspirational movie titles, a list of people you love, a list of things you love about yourself, or times that you laughed or smiled the hardest. You will be able to reference what you've written here to help you through your tough moments.

_____

_____

_____

_____

_____

_____

About the Author

As someone who was diagnosed with depression, I know how hard the mental battle can be. I've witnessed attempts and I've heard cries for help. These experiences of mine and others have inspired me and given me a purpose.

www.ingramcontent.com/pod-product-compliance
Lightning Source LLC
LaVergne TN
LVHW011858060526
838200LV00054B/4414